This book is dedicated to Laura Feldman,
without her knowledge
and passion this would not have been possible.
This is my way of honouring your gift and saying the biggest
'THANK YOU' XXX

Laura's Dream

Written and Illustrated by Tenille Dowe

Copyright © 2025 Tenille Dowe

All rights reserved. No part of this book may be reproduced in any manner whatsoever without prior written permission of the publisher.

First Printing, 2025

Published by Creative Heart Connection
www.creativeheartconnection.com

ISBN: 978-1-7636536-8-9

In a sunlit place where magical clouds pause,
stands a palace called Little Ivory Haus.

Its towers are crystals, all purple and pink.
They sparkle at dusk and shine when you blink.

The breeze hums softly through windows wide,
as sunlight and shadows dance inside.

There's a library deep where the stories arrive,
and pages turn gently as magic comes alive.

It's a wonderland filled with creativity and flair,
not far but still rare,
a jewel in the sky with magic in the air.

Laura slept soundly beneath the moonlight,
dreaming of ways she could share her bright light.

Her gifts came to life in the soft, starry gleam.

How can she help others believe in their dream?

Laura, like a fairy godmother,
spreading her joyous light.
In her beautiful crystal palace,
Little Ivory Haus, where dreams take flight.

With a wave of her wand,
she shares wisdom, knowledge and grace.

Turning wishes into reality with one gentle touch.

Her gift, creating a sense of community and oneness,
connecting like-minded people from all over the globe.

Her pink and purple crystal palace glistens under the sun,
where magic and kindness make every day fun!

In Laura's mystical library dreams take flight.

Books hold wonders, bathed in soft light.

Each page is a portal to realms old and new,
where tales of magic and adventure brew.

Her shelves stacked high with stories untold,
whisper secrets as time unfolds.

Wander through aisles of dreams so bright,
within each book, the stars ignite.

In this magical haven, imaginations thrive.

A world of wonder in every book's embrace,
in this magical library, dreams find their place.

In the digital realm,
Laura weaves her magic bright.

With computers, technology and creativity,
she guides others to bring their ideas to light.

Her talents blend, knowledge, education and passion
forming an interconnected phenomenal bridge.

Connecting self-published authors worldwide,
where dreams peacefully reside.

To Little Ivory Haus, they come,
sharing stories, challenges, crafting worlds
and chasing dreams.
Little Ivory Haus is where imagination runs.

Laura unites souls with a creative spark,
she has built a haven for inspired spirits,
where every voice leaves its mark.

From her cozy home in Australia's embrace,
Laura spreads her magic across time and space.

With a spark of thought and a heart so kind,
she helps others' dreams unwind.

Her wisdom travels far and wide,
guiding souls with love
and passion as her guide.

One idea, one action, she knows the power,
to help dreams bloom like a radiant flower.

Inspiring hearts from every land,
Laura shows what one can do with a guiding hand.

Her work, a testament to the strength we find,
when we let our dreams and actions intertwine.

In her magical library,
a wooden horse stands tall.

Perched on the table, though wooden and small,
with eyes so wise, it silently guides.

A guardian spirit by Laura's side.

Her Grandfather's gift,
a watchful steed,
whispering tales of grace,
hope and need.

A young girl once wandered where few others looked.
Finding peace in the pages of her childhood picture book.

Each story she opened was quiet and kind,
filled with animals of every shape you could find.
A soft little shelter for her heart and mind.

While the world bustled on with its chatter and pace,
she found gentle wonder in that quiet place.

She turned to a page with a flick and a grin,
where a black and white kitten was tumbling in.

Its whiskers were twitching,
his eyes full of mischievous play.
It pounced on the petals, then darted away.

Her heart skipped a beat,
she was lost in delight.

All thanks to that kitten in black and white,
on the page of her favourite picture book.

With a soft little thud and no hint of dread,
it landed on its back in the middle of the flower bed.

In a busy world, the little girl found her way,
with her guinea pig, brightening each day.

Through play and touch,
her furry friend taught her much.

With compassion and cuddles,
she found peace and joy intertwined.
Her guinea pig's squeak brought comfort and cheer,
making troubles disappear.

Together they'd sit, in a bond so kind,
teaching the dark-haired little girl to unwind her mind.

Through warmth and cuddles snug,
she learned peace is in a gentle hug.

In her heart, where dreams take flight,
with colours and lines, she finds her light.

Her textas dance and her imagination soars.
Creating worlds where her spirit explores.
Reading was hard, but she didn't mind,
as her dreams of colourful picture books filled her
heart and mind.

Little did she know,
one day her visions would leap,
in a picture book she created,
her dreams released.

Through drawing, she discovers a wondrous space,
where dreams of connection and stories embrace.

With each stroke, her future unfolds bright,
her creative journey brimming with delight.

Each night, as the stars begin to gleam.
The little, dark-haired girl drifts into a dream.
Imagining herself in her favourite book's scene.

As the years swiftly fly,
life unfolds with grace.
Facing challenges that time cannot erase.

She remembers her dreams
from the days of her youth.

A picture book was her
the vision and truth.

Her hands started releasing through
written word and scattered thought.
Her heart began healing
and remained full of care,
remembering why she was there.

She discovered purpose and connection,
creating her first story to share.

With twelve years gone by,
and countless hours spent.

A dream took shape,
as if heaven-sent.

Yet one piece remained to make the dream whole,
learning to publish was the ultimate goal.

In this journey of stories,
where dreams come alive,
Laura's self-publishing course
was the key to let her creativity thrive.

Once a little dark-haired girl with dreams so grand.
She grew up, had a family, and took a stand.

Creativity sparked in her heart's core,
healing and growing, that opened new doors.

With Laura's gift,
her dreams took flight.
Her stories and art,
set free in the world's spotlight.

In work and family, love intertwines,
as she shares her journey,
her spirit and heart shines.

In pages bound by what is and was,
she captures her life's journey,
with love as the cause.

Through vibrant pictures and rhythmic verse,
her pain and challenge transformed
into triumphant purpose.

To help others know they're not alone,
each word and image becomes her stepping stone.

A story of hope, where her heart can heal and mend,
in a picture book, she extends her hand like a friend.

All because Laura had a dream,
a little spark in her eye.
To share her knowledge and let it fly.

A gift she held, deep in her heart,
to spread her wisdom,
her journey's start.

With passion and grace,
she'd brightly beam,
her dream was to teach,
to inspire, and reach a large team.

Through stories and lessons,
her voice would soar,
her gift to the world, forevermore.

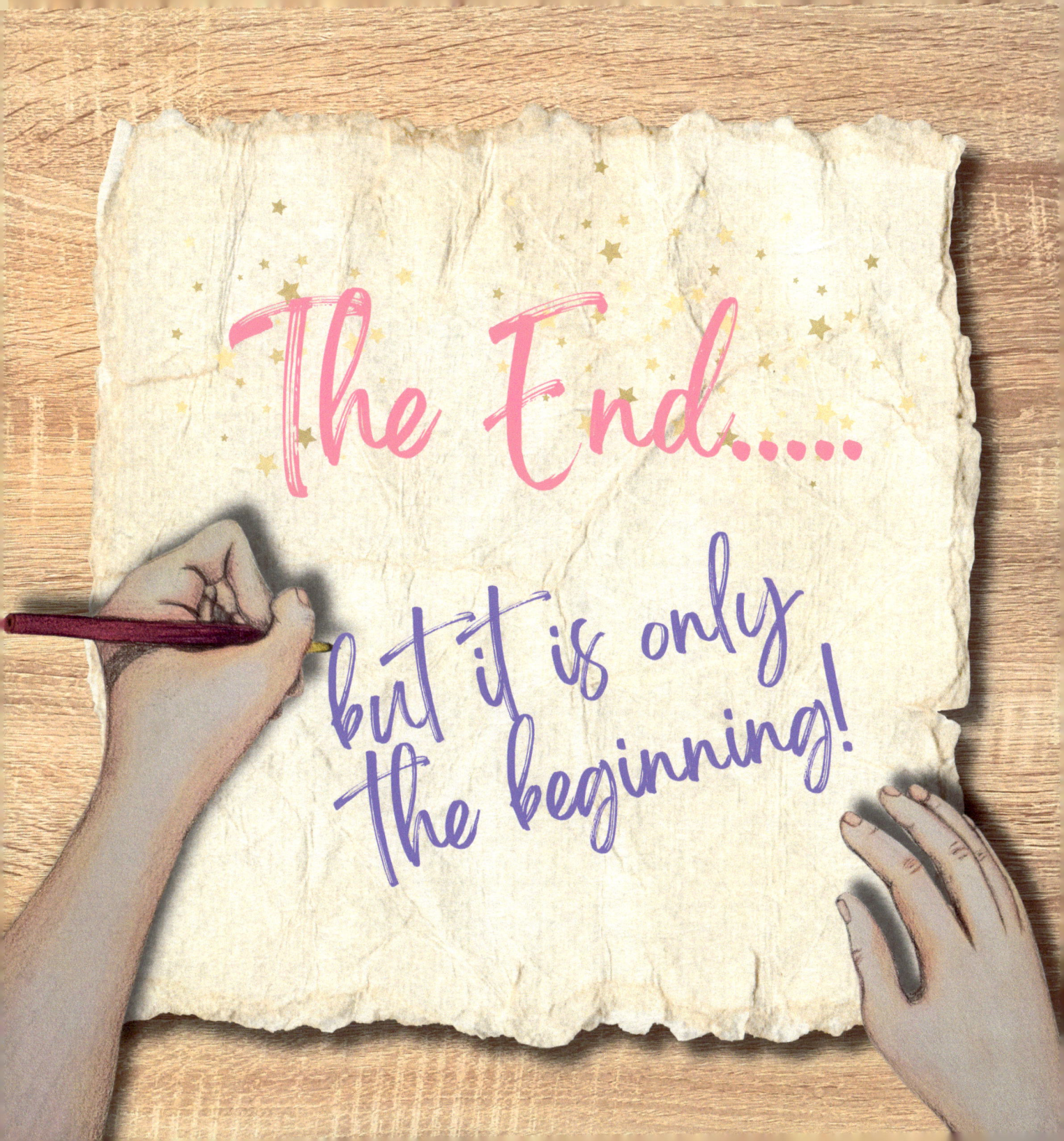

www.ingramcontent.com/pod-product-compliance
Lightning Source LLC
Chambersburg PA
CBHW041710160426
43209CB00018B/1791